Victory in Christ

Victory in Christ

Charles G. Trumbull

CHRISTIAN • LITERATURE • CRUSADE
Fort Washington, Pennsylvania 19034

CHRISTIAN LITERATURE CRUSADE
U.S.A.
P.O. Box 1449, Fort Washington, PA 19034

GREAT BRITAIN
51 The Dean, Alresford, Hants. SO24 9BJ

AUSTRALIA
P.O. Box 419M, Manunda, QLD 4879

NEW ZEALAND
10 MacArthur Street, Feilding

ISBN 0-87508-533-4

Copyright © 1959
The Sunday School Times Co.
Copyright assigned 1969 to
America's Keswick, Whiting, NJ 08759

This printing 2000

ALL RIGHTS RESERVED.

Printed in the United States of America

CONTENTS

1

WHAT IS YOUR KIND
OF CHRISTIANITY?

At a student missionary convention which I had the privilege of attending, we who were congratulating ourselves as being on somewhat higher ground than the ordinary church member in that we were willing to expend of our time, energy, and money to attend a missionary convention and share in our Lord's program for the evangelization of the world, were confronted over and over again, through one speaker after another, with a rather uncomfortable question, "Is your kind of Christianity worth sending to the non-Christian world?"

Not, "Is Christianity worth sending?" There is no question as to that. But what about your kind?—the kind that you showed by your life this morning, yesterday, last week, last year. Is *that* what the non-Christian world is waiting for, what is needed to revolutionize lives there?

Now there *is* a kind of Christianity worth sending to the non-Christian world. It is the

kind that Jesus Christ lives, the kind that He
has always lived. And the Christianity that
Christ Himself lives is the only kind worth
sending.

The kind of *salvation* that Jesus offers is
the only salvation worth offering to anyone.
So the kind of Christianity that Jesus lives,
moment by moment, is the only kind of
Christianity worth living.

We are sometimes helped by sheer coinci-
dences between our own experience and
some Scripture passage. We read about a
certain man who had been thirty and eight
years in his infirmity, and of whom Jesus
asked the question, "Wouldest thou be made
whole?" And then to whom, a moment later,
Jesus said, "Arise . . . and walk. And straight-
way the man was made whole, . . . and
walked."

That passage means a great deal to me.
For I know another man who for thirty and
eight years was in infirmity of spiritual
paralysis through his bondage to sin, and
who longed to be made whole; and to whom
our Lord one day said, "Arise, and walk." I
was a boy of about thirteen when I first
made public confession of Jesus Christ as my
Saviour; but it was not until twenty-five
years later that I even knew that Christ

offered to anyone in this life the power that He does offer for victory over sin. And I am convinced that many Christians, sincere believers in the Lord Jesus Christ as their personal Saviour, therefore regenerated, born again, nevertheless are in bondage and paralysis because, like myself, they have not known of our Lord's wonderful offer.

They are paralyzed, as I was, by the mistake of thinking that we ourselves must share in doing that which only God can do.

Jesus, you know, makes two offers to everyone. He offers to set us free from the *penalty* of our sin. And He offers to set us free from the *power* of our sin. Both these offers are made on exactly the same terms: we can accept them only by letting Him do it all.

Every Christian has accepted the first offer. Many Christians have not accepted the second offer. They mistakenly think, as I did, that they must have some part in overcoming the power of their sin; that their efforts, their will, their determination, strengthened and helped by the power of Christ, is the way to victory. And as long as they mistakenly believe this they are as doomed to defeat as they would be doomed to eternal death if their salvation depended upon their working with Christ to pay the penalty of their sin.

It has been well said that, while all true Christians know that they can have their justification only by faith, most of us have been brought up to believe that "for sanctification, we must paddle our own canoe." And that is why so many justified Christians are so pathetically, miserably disappointed in the matter of a satisfying, personal experience of sanctification, or walking "in newness of life."

Dr. Scofield in conversation was speaking of the up-and-down experience that so many Christians have, winning one day and failing the next, confessing their sins and trying again, and so going on in discouragement and defeat as a common experience. "That," said he, "is not Christian experience, but it is the experience of the Christian." And he went on to say that "Christian experience is wholly the result of the Producer of Christian experience: the Holy Spirit." So when Christians attempt to share in the work of producing their Christian experience, instead of letting the Holy Spirit do it all, they have the discouraging experience of many Christians—which is not Christian experience.

How did you accept Christ's offer of

freedom from the penalty of your sins? You took it as an outright gift. By faith you let Him do it all. Will you not accept His offer of immediate and complete freedom from the power of your known sins, on the same terms, and *do it now?* This is just as much a miracle as the miracle of regeneration. And it is just as exclusively the Lord's work.

A veteran missionary friend of mine told me a few years ago that he and some other missionaries in the foreign field, not a great while before that, had said to each other that their own daily lives were not of the sort described in the New Testament as character- istic of the early Christians. They did not know what the matter was; they only knew that they longed for something they did not have. And they agreed with each other to go apart by themselves for a few days if necessary, lay the whole matter before God and ask Him to give them what they did not have. They did this; God took them at their word; and my friend, consecrated Christian missionary and veteran in the service that he had already been, came back a new man in Christ, with a new life and with a new Christ.

He told another missionary, a high- spirited, high-tempered young woman, about the whole matter. She saw the truth, and was enabled of God to claim Christ in His fullness as her Victory, by faith, in the same way.

A few months later my friend, then at a distance from his younger missionary friend, received a letter from her in which she said that she must now tell him about the wonderful things that were going on in her life. "I wanted to write you at first," she said, "but I scarcely dared to, for I was afraid it would not last. But it *has* lasted, and oh, it is so wonderful! Why," she went on, "just as an illustration of what I mean, do you know that not only for three months have I not once slammed the door in the face of one of these stupid Indian servants that used to get on my nerves so, but I haven't even *wanted* to once in the three months!"

And that was a miracle. Not keeping from slamming the door—that is no miracle. Any ordinary, unsaved person who is half-way decent can keep from slamming the door: by setting his teeth, using his will, putting his hands behind his back, and determinedly not doing what he feels like doing. No, there is no miracle in *that*. But to go for three months without once *wanting* to: without once feeling within yourself that angry surge of irritation, of temper, that makes you want to show your feelings in some outward, uncontrolled way; does not your heart tell you that that indeed would be a miracle in your own life?

But that is Christ's offer to us now and here—freedom immediately and completely from all the power of known sin. That is what Paul meant as he came forever out of the seventh chapter of Romans into the eighth; when he said in the second verse of the eighth, "The law of the Spirit of life in Christ Jesus made me *free* from the law of sin and death" (A.S.V.). Are *you* rejoicing in Christ as your Victory in this miraculous way?

Do not misunderstand me; I am not speaking of any mistaken idea of sinless perfection. It is not possible for anyone to have such a transaction with Christ as to enable him to say, either, "I am without sin," or, "I can never sin again." This miracle is sustained and continued in our life only by our continuing, moment-by-moment faith in our Saviour for his moment-by-moment victory over the power of our sin. But He Himself will give us that faith, and will continue that faith in us moment by moment. We can and must, as Frances Ridley Havergal has so truly said, "entrust to Him our trust."

What are the conditions of this Victorious Life? Only two, and they are very simple. Surrender and faith. "Let go, and let God."

Some Christians have not surrendered unconditionally to the mastery of Jesus Christ. They have, as Mr. McConkey puts it, surrendered their sins to Christ, but not their wills. If there is anything in your life this moment that you know you have been withholding from the Lord, won't you give it to Him now? Won't you just tell Him you now turn over to Him, for time and eternity, all that you have and all that you are, for His complete mastery and use and disposal? Every habit of your life, every ambition, every hope, every loved one, every possession, and yourself—all these He must have if He is to make Himself not only your Saviour but your Life.

That is the first step, the first of the two conditions. But that is not the whole. Perhaps you made this surrender long ago, and have been wondering why you did not have the victory that you longed for. The reason is that the Surrendered Life is not necessarily the Victorious Life. There is no victory without surrender, but there may be surrender without victory. Some of us know this to our sorrow. We may have "let go," but if we have not yet "let God" we are sure to be defeated. We may not have realized that the work of victory is wholly and exclusively God's.

For after you have put yourself unreservedly and completely under the mastery of the Lord Jesus Christ, then you must know and remember that it at once becomes His responsibility, His—I say it reverently—duty, to keep you from the power of sin. He pledges Himself to do so. "Sin shall not have dominion over you," He says, "for ye are not under law" (where your works have something to do with it) "but under grace" (Rom. 6:14, A.S.V.) (where I do it all)—and elsewhere He adds, "My grace is sufficient for thee" (2 Cor. 12:9). So it is that our Lord has just been waiting for you, not to pray for victory, but to praise Him for victory. Many surrendered Christians postpone and prevent victory in their lives by praying for it, when Jesus has been waiting for them to praise Him for it. As one has said, we are not to ask Him to *make* His grace sufficient for us. He tells us that it is already so; and it is our part simply to take Him at His word and say, "I thank Thee, Lord."

Let us therefore claim the whole blessed miracle of the Victorious Life now, by saying this simple sentence together, prayerfully, thoughtfully, realizing the tremendous meaning of the words, and in our hearts praising God that it is true:

"I *know* that Jesus *is* meeting *all* my needs *now,* because His grace *is* sufficient for *me.*"

2

THE LIFE THAT WINS

There is only one life that wins; and that is the life of Jesus Christ. Every man may have that life; every man may live that life.

I do not mean that every man may be Christlike; I mean something very much better than that. I do not mean that a man may always have Christ's help; I mean something better than that. I do not mean that a man may have power from Christ; I mean something very much better than power. And I do not mean that a man shall be merely saved from his sins and kept from sinning; I mean something better than even that victory.

To explain what I do mean, I must simply tell you a very personal and recent experience of my own. I think I am correct when I say that I have known more than most men know about failure, about betrayals and dishonorings of Christ, about disobedience to heavenly visions, about conscious fallings short of that which I saw

other men attaining, and which I knew
Christ was expecting of me. Not a great
while ago I should have had to stop just
there, and only say I hoped that some day I
would be led out of all that into something
better. If you had asked me how, I would
have had to say I did not know. But, thanks
be to His long-suffering patience and infinite
love and mercy, I do *not* have to stop there,
but I can go on to speak of something more
than a miserable story of personal failure and
disappointment.

The conscious needs of my life, before
there came the new experience of Christ of
which I would tell you, were definite
enough. Three stand out.

1. There were great fluctuations in my
spiritual life, in my conscious closeness of
fellowship with God. Sometimes I would be
on the heights spiritually; sometimes I would
be in the depths. A strong, arousing convention, a stirring, searching address from some
consecrated, victorious Christian leader of
men; a searching, Spirit-filled book, or the
obligation to do a difficult piece of Christian
service myself, with the preparation in
prayer that it involved, would lift me up; and
I would stay up—for a while—and God would
seem very close and my spiritual life deep.

But it wouldn't last. Sometimes by some single failure before temptation, sometimes by a gradual downhill process, my best experiences would be lost, and I would find myself back on the lower levels. And a lower level is a perilous place for a Christian to be, as the Devil showed me over and over again.

It seemed to me that it ought to be possible for me to live habitually on a high plane of close fellowship with God, as I saw certain other men doing, and as I was not doing. Those men were exceptional, to be sure; they were in the minority among the Christians whom I knew. But I wanted to be in that minority. Why shouldn't we all be, and turn it into a majority?

2. Another conscious lack of my life was in the matter of failure before besetting sins. I was not fighting a winning fight in certain lines. Yet if Christ was not equal to a winning fight, what were my Christian beliefs and professions good for? I did not look for perfection. But I did believe that I could be enabled to win in certain directions habitually, yes, always, instead of uncertainly and interruptedly, the victories interspersed with crushing and humiliating defeats. Yet I had prayed, oh, so earnestly, for deliverance; and the habitual deliverance had not come.

3. A third conscious lack was in the matter of dynamic, convincing spiritual power that would work miracle changes in other men's lives. I was doing a lot of Christian work—had been at it ever since I was a boy of fifteen. I was going through the motions—oh, yes. So can anybody. I was even doing personal work—the hardest kind of all; talking with people, one by one, about giving themselves to my Saviour! *But I wasn't seeing results.* Once in a great while I would see a little in the way of result, of course; but not much. I didn't see lives made over by Christ, revolutionized, turned into firebrands for Christ themselves, because of my work; and it seemed to me I ought to. Other men did, why not I? I comforted myself with the old assurance (so much used by the Devil) that it wasn't for me to see results; that I could safely leave that to the Lord if I did my part. But this didn't satisfy me, and I was sometimes heartsick over the spiritual barrenness of my Christian service.

About a year before, I had begun, in various ways, to get intimations that certain men to whom I looked up as conspicuously blessed in their Christian service seemed to have a conception or consciousness of Christ that I did not have—that was beyond, bigger, deeper than any thought of Christ I had ever had. I rebelled at the suggestion when it first came to me. How *could* anyone have a better idea of Christ than I? (I am just laying bare to you the blind, self-satisfied workings of my sin-stunted mind and heart.) Did I not believe in Christ and worship Him as the Son of God and one with God? Had I not accepted Him as my personal Saviour more than twenty years before? Did I not believe that in Him alone was eternal life, and was I not trying to live in His service, giving my whole life to Him? Did I not ask His help and guidance constantly, and believe that in Him was my only hope? Was I not championing the very cause of the highest possible conception of Christ, by conducting in the columns of *The Sunday School Times* a symposium on the deity of Christ, in which the leading Bible scholars of the world were testifying to their personal belief in Christ as God? All this I was doing. How could a higher or better conception of Christ than mine be possible? I knew that I needed to *serve* Him far better than I had ever done; but that I needed a new conception of Him I would not admit.

And yet it kept coming at me, from directions that I could not ignore. I heard

from a preacher of power a sermon on
Ephesians 4:12, 13; "Unto the building up
of the body of Christ: till we all attain unto
the unity of the faith, and of the knowledge
of the Son of God, unto a fullgrown man,
unto the measure of the stature of the
fulness of Christ"; and as I followed it I was
amazed, bewildered. I couldn't follow him.
He was beyond my depth. He was talking
about Christ, unfolding Christ, in a way that
I admitted was utterly unknown to me.
Whether he was right or wrong I wasn't quite
ready to say that night; but if he *was* right,
then I was wrong.

Later I read another sermon by this same
man on "Paul's Conception of the Lord
Jesus Christ." As I read it, I was conscious of
the same uneasy realization that he and Paul
were talking about a Christ whom I simply
did not know. Could they be right? If they
were right, how could I get their knowledge?

One day I came to know another minister whose work among men had been
greatly blessed. I learned from him that what
he counted his greatest spiritual asset was his
habitual consciousness of the actual presence
of Jesus. Nothing so bore him up, he said, as
the realization that Jesus was *always* with
him in actual presence; and that this was so,

independent of his own feelings, independent of his deserts, and independent of his own notions as to how Jesus would manifest His presence. Moreover, he said that Christ was the home of his thoughts. Whenever his mind was free from other matters, it would turn to Christ; and he would talk aloud to Christ when he was alone—on the street, anywhere—as easily and naturally as to a human friend. So real to him was Jesus' presence.

Some months later I was in Edinburgh, attending the World Missionary Conference, and I saw that one whose writings had helped me greatly was to speak to men Sunday afternoon on "The Resources of the Christian Life." I went eagerly to hear him. I expected him to give us a series of definite things that we could do to strengthen our Christian life; and I knew I needed them. But his opening words showed me my mistake, while they made my heart leap with a new joy. What he said was something like this:

"The resources of the Christian life, my friends, are just—Jesus Christ."

That was all. But that was enough. I hadn't grasped it yet; but it was what all these men had been trying to tell me. Later, as I talked with the speaker about my personal needs and difficulties, he said, earnestly and simply, "Oh, Mr. Trumbull, if we would only step out upon Christ in a more daring faith, He could do so much more for us."

THE TWO CONDITIONS
FOR ENTERING THAT LIFE

Before leaving Great Britain I was confronted once more with the thought that was beyond me, a Christ whom I did not yet know, in a sermon that a friend of mine preached in his London church on a Sunday evening in June. His text was Philippians 1:21, "To me to live is Christ." It was the same theme—the unfolding of "the life that is Christ," Christ as the whole life and the only life. I did not understand all that he said, and I knew vaguely that I did not have as my own what he was telling us about. But I wanted to read the sermon again, and I brought the manuscript away with me when I left him.

It was about the middle of August that a crisis came with me. I was attending a young people's missionary conference, and was faced by a week of daily work there for which I knew I was miserably, hopelessly unfit and incompetent. For the few weeks previous had been one of my periods of spiritual letdown, not uplift, with all the loss and failure and defeat that such a time is sure to record.

The first evening that I was there a missionary bishop spoke to us on the Water of Life. He told us that it was Christ's wish and purpose that every follower of His should be a wellspring of living, gushing water of life *all the time* to others, not intermittently, not interruptedly, but with continuous and irresistible flow. We have Christ's own word for it, he said, as he quoted, "He that believeth on me, from within him shall flow *rivers* of living water." He told how some have a little of the water of life, bringing it up in small bucketfuls and at intervals, like the irrigating water wheel of India, with a good deal of creaking and grinding; while from the lives of others it flows all the time in a life-bringing, abundant stream that nothing can stop. And he described a little old native woman in the East whose marvelous ministry in witnessing for Christ put to shame those of us who listened. Yet she had known Christ for only a year.

The next morning, Sunday, alone in my room, I prayed it out with God, as I asked

Him to show me the way out. If there was a conception of Christ that I did not have, and that I needed because it was the secret of some of these other lives I had seen or heard of, a conception better than any I had yet had, and beyond me, I asked God to give it to me. I had with me the sermon I had heard, *"To me to live is Christ,"* and I rose from my knees and studied it. Then I prayed again. And God, in His long-suffering patience, forgiveness, and love, gave me what I asked for. He gave me a new Christ—wholly new in the conception and consciousness of Christ that now became mine.

Wherein was the change? It is hard to put it into words, and yet it is, oh, so new, and real, and wonderful, and miracle-working in both my own life and the lives of others.

To begin with, I realized for the first time that the many references throughout the New Testament to Christ in you, and you in Christ, Christ our life, and abiding in Christ, are literal, actual, blessed fact, and not figures of speech. How the 15th chapter of John thrilled with new life as I read it now! And the 3rd of Ephesians, 14 to 21. And Galatians 2:20. And Philippians 1:21.

What I mean is this: I had always known that Christ was my Saviour; but I had looked

upon Him as an external Saviour, one who
did a saving work *for* me from outside, as it
were; one who was ready to come close
alongside and stay by me, helping me in all
that I needed, giving me power and strength
and salvation. But now I knew something
better than that. At last I realized that Jesus
Christ was actually and literally within me;
and even more than that: that He had
constituted Himself my very life, taking me
into union with Himself—my body, mind,
and spirit—while I still had my own identity
and free will and full moral responsibility.
Was not this better than having Him as a
helper, or even than having Him as an
external Saviour: to have Him, Jesus Christ,
God the Son, as my own very life? It meant
that I need never again ask Him to help me
as though He were one and I another; but
rather simply to do His work, His will, in me,
and with me, and through me. My body was
His, my mind His, my will His, my spirit His;
and not merely His, but literally a part of
Him; what He asked me to recognize was, "I
have been crucified with Christ, and it is no
longer I that live, but Christ liveth in me."
Jesus Christ had constituted Himself my
life—not as a figure of speech, remember, but
as a literal, actual fact, as literal as the fact

that a certain tree has been made into this desk on which my hand rests. For "your bodies are members of Christ"; and "ye are the body of Christ."

Do you wonder that Paul could say with tingling joy and exultation, "To me to live is Christ"? He did not say, as I had mistakenly been supposing I must say, "To me to live is to be Christ-like," nor, "To me to live is to have Christ's help," nor, "To me to live is to serve Christ." No; he plunged through and beyond all that in the bold, glorious, mysterious claim, "To me to live *is* Christ." I had never understood that verse before. Now, thanks to His gift of Himself, I am beginning to enter into a glimpse of its wonderful meaning.

And that is how I know for myself that there is a life that wins: that it is the life of Jesus Christ: and that it may be our life for the asking, if we let Him—in absolute, unconditional surrender of ourselves to Him, our wills to His will, making Him the Master of our lives as well as our Saviour—enter in, occupy us, overwhelm us with Himself, yea, fill us with Himself "unto all the fulness of God."

What has the result been? Did this experience give me only a new intellectual conception of Christ, more interesting and satisfying than before? If it were only that, I should have little to tell you today. No; it meant a revolutionized, fundamentally changed life, within and without. If any man be *in Christ,* you know, there is a new creation.

Do not think that I am suggesting any mistaken, unbalanced theory that, when a man receives Christ as the fullness of his life, he cannot sin again. The "life that is Christ" still leaves us our free will; with that free will we can resist Christ; and my life, since the new experience of which I speak, has recorded sins of such resistance. But I have learned that the restoration after failure can be supernaturally blessed, instantaneous, and complete. I have learned that, as I trust Christ in surrender, there need be no fighting against sin, but complete freedom from the power and even the desire of sin. I have learned that this freedom, this more than conquering, is sustained in unbroken continuance as I simply recognize that Christ is my cleansing, reigning life.

The three great lacks or needs of which I spoke at the opening have been miraculously met.

1. There has been a fellowship with God

utterly differing from and infinitely better than anything I had ever known in all my life before.

2. There has been an utterly new kind of victory, victory-by-freedom, over certain besetting sins—the old ones that used to throttle and wreck me—when I have trusted Christ for this freedom.

3. And, lastly, the spiritual results in service have given me such a sharing of the joy of Heaven as I never knew was possible on earth. Six of my most intimate friends, most of them mature Christians, soon had their lives completely revolutionized by Christ, laying hold on Him in this new way and receiving Him unto all the fullness of God. Two of these were a mother and a son, the son a young businessman twenty-five years old. Another was the general manager of one of the large business houses in Philadelphia. Though consecrated and active as a Christian for years, he began letting Christ work out through him in a new way into the lives of his many associates, and of his salesmen all over the country. A white-haired man of over seventy found a peace in life and a joy in prayer that he had long ago given up as impossible for him. Life fairly teems with the miracle-evidences of what

Christ is willing and able to do for other lives through anyone who just turns over the keys to His complete indwelling.

Jesus Christ does not want to be our helper; He wants to be our life. He does not want us to work for Him. He wants us to let Him do His work through us, using us as we use a pencil to write with—better still, using us as one of the fingers on His hand.

When our life is not only Christ's, but Christ, our life will be a winning life; for He cannot fail. And a winning life is a fruit-bearing life, a serving life. It is after all only a small part of life, and a wholly negative part, to overcome; we must also bear fruit in character and in service if Christ is our life. And we shall—because Christ is our life. "He cannot deny himself"; He "came not to be ministered unto, but to minister." An utterly new kind of service will be ours now, as we let Christ serve others through us, using us. And this fruit bearing and service, habitual and constant, must all be by faith in Him; our works are the result of His Life in us; not the condition, or the secret, or the cause of that Life.

The conditions of thus receiving Christ as the fullness of the life are simply two—after, of course, our personal acceptance of Christ

as our Saviour—through His shed blood and
death as our Substitute and Sin-Bearer—from
the guilt and consequences of our sin.

1. Surrender absolutely and unconditionally to Christ as Master of all that we are
and all that we have, telling God that we are
now ready to have His whole will done in
our entire life, at every point, no matter
what it costs.

2. Believe that God has set us wholly
free from the law of sin (Rom. 8:2)—not *will*
do this, but *has* done it. Upon this second
step, the quiet act of faith, all now depends.
Faith must believe God in entire absence of
any feeling or evidence. For God's word is
safer, better, and surer than any *evidence* of
His word. We are to say, in blind, cold faith
if need be, "I *know* that my Lord Jesus *is*
meeting *all* my needs *now* (even my need of
faith), because His grace *is* sufficient for
me."

And remember that Christ Himself is
better that any of His blessings; better than
the power, or the victory, or the service that
He grants. Christ creates spiritual power; but
Christ is better than that power. He is God's
best: we may have Christ, yielding to Him in
such completeness and abandonment of self
that it is no longer we that live, but Christ
that liveth in us. Will you thus take Him?

3

REAL AND COUNTERFEIT VICTORY

Victory is a great word in the New Testament, and yet I am sure there are many Christians who have received Jesus as Saviour, who have been born again and have passed from death unto life, who nevertheless are deceived day by day by a counterfeit victory when God wants them to know what real victory is. I can speak with deep feeling as to this, because I lived to be nearly forty years old (after having lived for more than twenty-five years as a sincere Christian) never knowing what real victory was, and having all those years taken the counterfeit victory—active Christian worker though I was—as a substitute for the real.

Our Lord once said to some Jews, who were sure that they were all right, "Every one that committeth sin is the bondservant of sin . . . . If therefore the Son shall make you free, ye shall be free indeed"(John 8:34-36)

Then again, the same Holy Spirit who

indwelt the Lord Jesus said to Paul, "Sin shall not have dominion over you: for ye are not under law, but under grace," and the Lord Himself adds later, "My grace is sufficient for thee." "Ye are not under law" which says DO, "but under grace" which says DONE, and that is the reason why "sin shall not have dominion over you." So it is that Paul could cry out to the Galatians, as he was making that passionate protest against relapsing from grace into law, as most of us Christians have done at one time or another, "I have been crucified with Christ, and it is no longer I that live, but Christ liveth in me." And again in Philippians, "To me to live is Christ." And to the Corinthians, "Thanks be to God, who giveth us the victory through our Lord Jesus Christ." If there is one word that we do not always realize should be printed in capital letters in that triumphant thanksgiving, it is the word "GIVETH." "Thanks be to God, who GIVETH us the victory through our Lord Jesus Christ." That is grace. That is the test of the real or the counterfeit victory. Just remember this: any victory over the power of any sin whatsoever in your life that you have to get by working for it is counterfeit. Any victory that you have to get by trying for it is counterfeit. If you have to work for your victory, it is not the real thing; it is not the thing that God offers you.

On the train this afternoon I was reading a letter from a woman who is at this Convention, and she said, "I am trying to live the victorious life, and so I" did so and so under certain circumstances. That Christian friend may be in this audience tonight; and if she is, I cannot refrain from saying that as long as she keeps on trying to live the victorious life, she won't live it. If any of you are making the mistake of trying to live the victorious life, you are cheating yourself out of it, for the victory you get by trying for it is a counterfeit victory. You must substitute another word; not try, but trust, and you cannot try and trust at the same time. Trying is what we do, and trusting is what we let the Lord do.

Let us think for a few minutes of concrete examples of the counterfeit victory and the real victory, keeping in mind as we do so the offer of the Lord Jesus to set us free so that we shall be free indeed. Because the pity of it, the tragedy of it, is that the Christian people of our land have not been taught the truth in this matter. Our Ministers, many of them, are not able to teach the truth in this matter. They themselves have not been taught the truth. Our seminaries are not teaching it. So laymen and ministers are substituting counterfeit victory for the real.

I read not long ago some extracts from a sermon by a well-known preacher, and they were something like this: "We all of us need to do weeding, rooting up the bad weeds in the garden of our own life. The thing to do is to give your attention to some weed, some sin that has taken root in your life, and with prayer and effort dig it up. It may take you a long time, but keep at it day after day, week after week, month after month if necessary, till you have weeded that sin out. After you have gotten rid of that sin, take another, and keep at that till you have weeded it out. And then another and another of the sins of your life, till you have made your garden what it ought to be."

Dear friends, you do not find anything of this sort in God's Word. A victory gained in that way, by a gradual conquest over evil, getting one sin after another out of our life, is *counterfeit* victory. No, the Lord Jesus does not offer to give us any such gradual victory over the sins of our life.

There is an old story, which I am very

sure is not a true one, but a very good one to remember because it illustrates so clearly the mistake of supposing that victory over our own sins can at best be only gradual. A man who was down and out wandered into a rescue mission one night, and there found Jesus Christ as his Saviour. He had been a thief, but now he was saved. As he went out from the mission, he talked with himself something like this: "I have been a thief, a pickpocket. When business was good, I have picked on an average a dozen pockets a day. But now I am a Christian, and I must give up that method of earning my livelihood. For the rest of this week I will reduce that number of pockets to about eight a day, for I am a Christian now. The week after that I will cut it down to about six a day. During the third week I shall not be picking more than three or four pockets a day, and in a month from now I shall have given it up entirely, for I am a Christian now."

I don't believe that is a true story, do you? I don't believe that a man who had found Christ as his Saviour would be so foolish as to reason with himself that way about the sin of thieving. But, dear friends, I have an idea that I am looking into the faces of some Christian people who have been just foolish enough to reason that way about the known sins of *their* life; that next year, and the year after, and the year after that, they would have reduced some of the known sins of their life until sometime in the vague future they would have given them up entirely. And I am perfectly sure that *you* are looking into the face of a man who was foolish enough to reason that way about the sins of his life for many years.

No! the victorious life, the life of freedom from the power of sin, is not a gradual gift. There is no such thing as a gradual gift. And victory is a gift. It is not a growth. "Thanks be unto God who GIVETH us the victory through our Lord Jesus Christ." How long does it take you to grow into your Christmas presents? On Christmas morning, when you come downstairs, and find them there on the table with your name on them, how long does it take you to grow into those gifts? One minute a gift is not yours, though it is labeled with your name. The next minute it is yours. Why? Because in that minute you have *taken* it. You did not grow into it; in an instant you took it. Victory is a gift which we take in exactly the same way.

Please do not misunderstand me as saying that in the victorious life there is no growth. That would be absolutely false; wholly untrue to the Word of God. But we only begin to grow normally, grow as God wants us to grow, after we have entered into victory. Then we have the chance to grow for the first time as we ought to grow. And then we can "grow in grace" in a thousand and one ways; grow as long as we live, learning more of the Lord all the time, and of His Word, and growing as He wants us to grow; but not growing in freedom from the power of sin. For we can have that victory today as completely as we can ever have it in this world. If Jesus is not able to do it for us today, then He will never be able to do it for us. But, praise God, He is! And He is "the same yesterday, and today, and for ever."

Victory is not fighting down your wrong desires. That is counterfeit victory. It is not concealing your wrong feelings. That is the counterfeit. Yet, how many of us have supposed that victory is simply keeping our wrong feelings from expressing themselves. Do you remember the story of the old Quaker lady, told over and over again to illustrate victory? This dear old Quaker lady, who apparently never lost her temper, always keeping unruffled under the most trying circumstances, was approached one day by a young girl friend, who said: "I want you to tell me *how* under the sun you do it. How do you always keep sweet the way you do? Why, if some of the things happened to me that I have seen happen to you, I would just boil over; but you never do."

And the old Quaker lady answered quietly, "Perhaps I don't boil over, my dear, but thee doesn't know what boiling is going on inside."

That story has been told as an example of wonderful Christian victory. It is no such thing. It is a counterfeit; it is a fake; it denies the offer of the Word of God. If the only victory we can have is to be boiling inside and not let people know how sinful we feel, that is a poor kind of victory. The Lord Jesus Christ never offered it to anyone. For it does not take any supernatural grace to keep from boiling over if you are boiling inside. Anybody can do that if there is inducement enough. Any businessman who wants to sell goods, or to get another man to sign a business contract so that he can make money—if the man he is talking to says something that makes him "boil inside," he is not going to boil over. It is not good business. He smiles, and for purely selfish reasons he does not let the other know how he feels. But there is no grace, no miracle, no victory in that. Anybody can keep from boiling over, I say. Women do it all the time for social reasons—and there is no Christianity, no grace in that.

But I heard of a woman who did not "boil over" for a very different reason. She was out in India as a missionary. She had gone out there to serve Christ; doubtless she was a surrendered Christian. But she was not yet a victorious Christian. Perhaps we do not realize that surrender and victory are not always the same thing. It is possible to be a completely surrendered Christian and a defeated Christian, as some of you may know to your sorrow. An older missionary friend of the younger missionary told of her experience himself. One day he with other missionary friends said, "We are not living the kind of life that the New Testament describes and that those early Christians apparently lived. Let us go away by ourselves and ask God to show us what is the matter, and to give us what we have not got." They dropped their work and went off for a few days, asking for they knew not what, but hungry for what they did not have. And God met them, and gave them what they asked for. They came back changed men, with

Christ in His fullness reigning in their hearts,
and with *the* victory. Then this older missionary told the younger woman about it. He
told her of the revolution wrought in his life,
veteran missionary though he was. She saw
the truth and took it all by faith.

Some months later, he—then at a
distance—had a letter from her saying that
she must now tell him of the wonderful
things that were happening in her life, so
wonderful, she said, that she could scarce
believe they were true. "I wanted to write
you at first," she said, "but I was afraid it
would not last. But it has lasted. For
example, do you know that for three months
now I have not only not once slammed the
door in the face of one of these stupid
Indian servants that used to get on my nerves
so, but I haven't even *wanted* to, once in the
three months?"

That was a miracle. That was victory. It
is not a miracle to go without slamming the
door for three months. We can put our hands
behind our back, set our teeth, and not slam
the door. But would it be a miracle for you
to go three months without ever once feeling
within your heart that angry surge of irritation, impatience, unlove, that would make it
a relief to "slam the door" or give expression

in some way to your feelings? Would *that* be a miracle? Yes, our hearts tell us that it would. We know that no effort of our own can possibly bring such a miracle to pass; the taking away from our hearts of even the "want to" of sinful desire. That young woman now had real victory, the miracle, the gift of victory, which can never be wrought by our will power or resolution, or by our efforts of any sort.

Dear friends, *that* is the real thing. That is real victory. In the counterfeit victory we have to conceal how we feel. The counterfeit victory means a struggle; whatever we do, we do by our efforts. Oh, yes, we ask Him to help us, and then we feel that we must do a lot to help Him—as if He needed to be helped! In real victory, He does it all. We do not dare to help. We realize that the battle is His. And remembering that Christ is our life, we do not need to conceal Christ. The things we have to conceal in our lives are the things that are from Satan, not from Christ; from our sinful nature, not from our "born again" nature.

When the Lord Jesus Christ by the Holy Spirit works in our life to give us this victory, it is a miracle every time. If it is not a miracle, it is not victory. Yet that is the man who had said a few days before, "If you say that is true of you, I believe you; but it never could be true of me."

Yes, it can be true of anyone whom God has created. The Redeemer Christ can be our victory. It is not a matter of temperament or environment; it is a matter of Jesus Christ, and it is *His* grace that is sufficient.

4

IS VICTORY EARNED, OR A GIFT?

Every saved child of God at one time or another longs for victory over sin. Yet many such children of God have sadly given up hope of having in this world a complete victory, mistakenly supposing that that blessing is only for the life after this. They do not know how simple, and how immediately available, is the victory for which they are not daring to hope. It is right at hand, in Christ, for all who let Him undeceive them as to the lie which Satan has told them, and who will receive the victorious life as the outright, supernatural gift of God.

An earnest Christian expresses what are more or less the thoughts of many on this subject. He writes with hearty appreciation, yet with frankly expressed positiveness:

Under the heading, "Victory Christ's Work, Not Ours," you state:

"Christ is living the victorious life today; and Christ is your life. Therefore stop trying. Let him do it all. Your effort or trying had nothing to do with the salvation which you have in Christ: in exactly the same way your effort and trying can have nothing to do with the complete victory which Christ alone has achieved for you and can steadily achieve in you."

Can this be true? If it is, why should anyone make the effort so much as to accept Christ as his Saviour, let alone striving to put out of his life tendencies that he knows are bad, that his life may be purer and better, more attractive and lovable? If Christ does it all, why so much as the effort even to believe that he is the Saviour?

You have taken the incentive to be a Christian out of the hands of anyone by saying that Christ saves whom He will regardless of whether they want to be saved or not, or you are preaching the Gospel of universal salvation.

I have no hesitancy in saying I do not believe in your position. My entire experience refutes it. Had I never made the effort to be a child of God through Christ, and desired it and agonized that I might be saved, I do not believe that I should ever have had the consciousness of being saved by Him, but probably would have gone on as a selfish and self-seeking man of the world, and paid less and less attention to His claims upon my life. Therefore I claim that Christ plus my efforts won the victory—either futile without the other.

I believe that the victorious life which your correspondent writes about is brought about by the continuous desire and effort to gain it, and that it will not come without that desire and that effort. I realize, of course, that no man can save himself, but I believe that God expects every man to do his part toward that salvation.

It is true that God can save no man unless that man does his part toward salvation. But what is man's part? It is to receive the salvation that God offers him in Christ. *The Sunday School Times* is not preaching Universalism. It believes that the whole message of the Bible rebukes that mistake. God forces salvation on no one; and God has revealed to us in His Word that many reject salvation. Our wills are free to act; their action is the accepting or the rejecting of the "free gift of God ... eternal life in Christ Jesus our Lord."

But this act of the will, by which we voluntarily and deliberately decide to take what God offers us, is not what was meant, in that editorial on victory, by "effort." Men do not, by agonized effort, secure their salvation. They may agonize indeed under the conviction of sin which the Holy Spirit brings into their life. That is His way of showing them that they need salvation. But their agony ceases when they accept the free gift and realize that God has done for them what, by all their agony, they could never have done for themselves.

Yet the great truth that so many earnest, surrendered Christians have even yet failed to see is that salvation is a twofold gift;

freedom from the *penalty* of sin, and freedom from the *power* of sin. All Christians have received in Christ as their Saviour their freedom from the penalty of their sins, and they have received this as an outright gift from God. But many Christians have not yet realized that they may, in the same way, and by the same kind of faith in the same God and Saviour, receive now and here the freedom from the power of their sins which was won for them by their Saviour on the cross and in His resurrection victory. Even though they know clearly that their own efforts have nothing to do with their salvation from the *penalty* of their sins, they are yet deceived by the Adversary into believing that somehow their own efforts must play a part in their present victory over the *power* of their sins. *Our efforts can not only never play any part in our victory over the power of sin, but they can and do effectually prevent such victory.*

If an unsaved man came to Christ, and said, "I want to be saved from the penalty of my sins, and I will let You save me provided You will let me share in accomplishing my salvation, so that You and I shall always know that You did part of it and I did part of it," Christ could not save that man.

Salvation is a gift; and a gift is not a gift if it is partly earned.

In exactly the same way, if we, as saved Christians, come to our Lord and say, "I want to be saved from the power of my sins, and I will let You save me provided You will let me share with You in the work of overcoming their power, so that You and I shall always know that part of this victory has been accomplished by You, and part has been accomplished by me," Christ cannot save us from the power of our sins. When our Lord says to us by the Holy Spirit through Paul, "Sin shall not have dominion over you: for ye are not under law, but under grace," He wants us to remember what grace is. Grace is not partly man's work and partly God's work. It is wholly God's work and exclusively God's work; and all that man can do is to receive it as God's outright, unde-served, and wholly sufficient gift.

We are to use our will to accept the gift of victory; we are not to make an effort to win the victory. What should we say of children in a household who spent Christmas Eve agonizing in their desires and efforts to make sure that on the morrow they should have all the gifts that Christmas ought to bring them? Would this be pleasing to the

loving parents who had been spending themselves to the uttermost of their resources to
provide gifts for those children? Even supposing that on Christmas morning the children stopped their agonizing and their efforts, and gratefully took from the open,
loving hands of their parents all that was
being offered to them: what part would the
struggles of the night before have played in
the receiving of the gifts? At the best would
it not have been, not only utterly unnec-
essary, but a sad reflection on the trust-
worthiness and love of the parents? And
could not the receiving of the gifts take place
only after the mistaken efforts had ceased?

The only thing for those children to do
on Christmas Day is to use their wills to
receive what the love of the parents has
provided. If a child chose to use this will to
refuse the gifts, the gifts would not be his.
There would be no "universalism," even in
that little family, if a gift was deliberately
refused by a child. But the efforts of the
children can have no place in making Christmas Day a time of their joyous receiving of
the expressed love of the father and mother.

Our Lord wants our lives on earth to be
one long Christmas Day of receiving His gift
of Himself as our victory. We don't need to

agonize about it; we don't need to work for it. The more we work and the more we agonize, the more we prevent or postpone what He wants to give us now. If we say that our experience refutes this, do we mean that we have found through the help of our own efforts a satisfying completeness of victory in our life over all recognized sin, so that impatience, irritation, unlove, impurity, have been taken out of our life, and we are able to live from day to day not only free from outward expression of these sins, but free from their dominion within us? Perhaps we have not even dared to hope for the freedom that Christ is really offering us now and here from the power of known sin.

The effortless life is not the will-less life. We use our will to believe, to receive, but not to exert effort in trying to accomplish what only God can do. Our hope for victory over sin is not "Christ plus my efforts," but "Christ plus my receiving." To receive victory from Him is to believe His word that solely by His grace He is, this moment, freeing us from the dominion of sin. And to believe on Him in this way is to recognize that He is doing for us what we cannot do for ourselves. When our Lord was in Nazareth He could do "not many mighty works there because of "—their inactivity? No; "because of their unbelief." Christ's power is not futile without our effort, but it is made futile by our effort. To attempt to share by our effort in what only grace can do is to defeat grace. "This only would I learn from you, Received ye the Spirit by the works of the law, or by the hearing of faith? Are ye so foolish? having begun in the Spirit, are ye now perfected in the flesh? . . . He therefore that supplieth to you the Spirit, and worketh miracles among you, doeth he it by the works of the law, or by the hearing of faith? . . . For freedom did Christ set us free: Stand fast therefore, and be not entangled again in the yoke of bondage. . . . But I say, Walk by the Spirit, and ye shall not fulfil the lust of the flesh" (Gal. 3:2, 3, 5; 5:1, 16).

The victorious life is brought about wholly by Christ, and is sustained, not by our continued effort, but through our continued receiving.

And let us never forget this simple truth: the faith which lets Christ bring us into and sustain us in victory is just remembering that Christ is faithful; that it is *His* responsibility and duty to accomplish this miracle in our lives, and that He is always true to His duty.

5

VICTORY WITHOUT TRYING

A question recently came to *The Sunday School Times* office: "What do you consider the most dangerous heresy of today?" I wonder what answer you would have made. Perhaps you think there are so many heresies that it is hard to say which is the most dangerous. Would you have said Christian Science, the Higher Criticism, New Theology, Millennial Dawnism? Any one of those things is dangerous enough. But none of these, I believe, is the most dangerous heresy of today. For the most dangerous is the emphasis that is being given, right in the professing Christian church itself, on *what we do for God,* instead of on *what God does for us.*

Oh, I hope God will make that very plain to us! As you go out from this Institute into your ministry, whatever form it takes, you will realize the subtle, almost all-pervading presence of that thing: the emphasis in the church, and in Christian organizations, on

what we do for God as the great thing, as the
most important thing; instead of just the
opposite—the emphasis as we ought to place
it, on what God does for us.

You hear people saying, "Get busy for
God, and the rest will take care of itself."
Even in evangelistic services, even in revivals
where the blood of Christ is rightly being
pointed to as the only way of salvation, you
have heard that mistaken emphasis, the call
to "Be a man" if you would get saved. In a
great evangelistic revival where souls were
being saved, I have heard the evangelist cry
out, as he called upon men to hit the trail
and come up and acknowledge Jesus Christ
as Saviour, "Be a man! Don't be a milk-sop!
Don't be a mollycoddle! Be a man!"

But there is no such call in the Bible to
the unsaved; God never tells one to "assert
his manhood" by accepting Christ. The
offense of the cross is just the opposite. It is
a degrading thing, a humiliating thing, to
recognize why the cross saves. I do not mean
that the cross degrades us, but that the cross
exposes our degradation; it humiliates us
into the dust. There is no Scripture appeal to
the unsaved to "be a man and accept
Christ"; but there is a clear declaration from
God that, because you are less than a man,

less than a woman, because there is no hope
in you, because you are dead in trespasses
and sins, you must let God save you through
the death of Christ as your slain substitute.
You can't do anything for yourself. No;
salvation is not asserting our manhood;
salvation is recognizing our utter lack of
manhood and womanhood, our hopelessness,
our worthlessness; recognizing that, if we are
to be saved, it has got to be done for us by
God.

May God make very plain to us all in this
hour something about the grace of God. This
mistaken emphasis of today looks in exactly
the opposite direction from grace. It looks in
the direction of works. Not that works have
no place in the Christian's life. You know
they have. But they *follow* the grace of God;
they do not precede it; and they are never
the condition of God's grace.

I heard a Christian say, a few years ago,
that he supposed very few Christians had any
intelligent idea of the meaning of grace. And
do you know, I was indignant at that! I said
to myself: "That's nonsense! It's not true,
that very few Christians have any intelligent
idea of grace. Every saved person knows
perfectly well what grace is." But I have
come to see my mistake. I did not know

much about grace when I was so indignant at
the suggestion that most Christians do not.
But God, in His infinite grace and patience
has been showing me more and more of the
infinite, unsearchable riches of the meaning
of that word GRACE. And now I realize that
I still know very little of the meaning of
grace; and that, so far as most Christians are
concerned, the lack of knowledge is pitiable
and tragic.

Will you let me remind you of three
things that God's grace does for us?

In the first place, What is grace? We all
know that it is God's beneficent work for us,
wholly independent of what we are and what
we do. It is not merely God's *attitude*
toward us, but His *activity* in our behalf.
Grace does not mean that God stands off
and smilingly looks in our direction. Grace
means His tremendous, omnipotent activity;
the dynamite of Heaven accomplishing
things in our behalf, wholly independent of
what we are and of what we do.

And what is God's threefold work of
grace for us?

I am going to take the third first, of
three great things that God's grace does for
us. In Romans 8:21 we read this: "Because
the creature itself also shall be delivered

from the bondage of corruption into the glorious liberty of the children of God." In 1 Corinthians 15:51, 52 we read: "Behold, I show you a mystery; We shall not all sleep, but we shall all be changed, in a moment, in the twinkling of an eye, at the last trump: for the trumpet shall sound, and the dead shall be raised incorruptible, and we shall be changed." And in 1 Thessalonians 4:16, 17: "For the Lord himself shall descend from heaven with a shout, with the voice of the archangel, and with the trump of God: and the dead in Christ shall rise first: then we which are alive and remain shall be caught up together with them in the clouds, to meet the Lord in the air: and so shall we ever be with the Lord."

Those three passages tell us one thing that God's grace accomplishes for us; and here are three great facts about the same work of grace—creation shall be delivered; the dead shall be raised; and we that are alive shall be caught up. The resurrection of the body; the deliverance from the general bondage of corruption in which all creation is at this time; and our blessed hope of being caught up to meet the Lord in the air.

Now did you notice that all three of those great verbs are in the passive voice, not the active? It does not say that creation shall deliver itself from corruption. They shall *be* delivered. The verb is passive. Nor does it say, "The dead shall raise themselves." It has to be done for them. And it does not say, "We shall spring up in the air to meet the Lord," but, "We shall be caught up." It all has to be done for us; it is God's grace, not man's works.

When I was a young fellow in college I went in a little for the high jump. I was a proud youngster when I won a prize cup in the freshman games at Yale for the running high jump. But suppose any of us got the idea that, at the time of the rapture, when the trump shall sound and the Lord shall come into the air to meet His saints, we had somehow to use our power to raise ourselves up out of this earth to meet the Lord. Suppose the best high jumpers thought they had a better chance for getting into the proper place to meet the Lord in the air, because of their skill in high jumping. Absurd, you say. Of course. But it isn't one bit more absurd than the mistake, dear friends, which I made about another part of the work of God's grace for us, during the first twenty-five years of my Christian life. I was a saved man for twenty-five years while I made the mistake of attempting to *help* God in a work which is exclusively of the grace of God—a mistake just as absurd as to suppose that any strength I used to have in the running high jump will be as useful on the day when the Lord called His Chruch to meet Him in the air.

There is another wonderful thing that God's grace does for us. It is the second of our three. We noted the last first; now let us take the first second. We find it in Ephesians 2:1: "You hath he made alive, who were dead in trespasses and sins; . . . God, who is rich in mercy, for his great love wherewith he loved us, even when we were dead in sins, made us alive together with Christ, (by grace ye are saved;) and hath raised us up together."

"Hath," The first word of grace that we noted, God is going to do in the future. He *will* raise up the dead and change the living. But now Paul says, He *"hath* raised us up together, and made us sit together in heavenly places in Christ Jesus: that in the ages to come he might show the exceeding riches of his grace in his kindness toward us through Christ Jesus. For by grace are ye saved through faith; and that not of yourselves; it is the gift of God: not of works, lest

any man should boast" (Eph. 2:6-9). That seems to be grace according to God's idea. Thus the dead man is saved by the grace of God, by the work of God for him, not by anything he does; through simple faith in that finished and completed and unimprovably perfect work of God, he is born again.

How much of that work does God do? The most of it? Pretty nearly all of it? No! *All!* Grace does not *share* anything with man. Grace is not a joint effort. Grace is not co-operation. Grace is jealous—as God is a jealous God, grace is absolutely exclusive. Grace means "God does it all." And it was done for us nineteen centuries before we were born.

Grace shuts out our works, so far as our having any share in the work which grace accomplishes. Grace *results* in our works, in a most wonderful way, but our works do not help grace a bit. I remember how startled I was when I first had called to my attention those words in Romans 4:5, "To him that worketh not, but believeth on him that justifieth the ungodly, his faith is counted for righteousness." To him that *worketh not*—just keeps absolutely still and simply believes on Him that justifieth the ungodly, his faith is counted for righteousness. We had nothing to do with bearing the sins of the world, did we? And we had nothing to do with bearing our own sins. They have been borne for us, taken away. "Behold the Lamb of God, which taketh away the sin of the world." That's grace. That's why grace says "Done: Finished!"

GOD'S GRACE IN THE BELIEVER'S PRESENT LIFE

Now for the third thing that grace does. This third in the order in which we are taking them is the second, or the middle part, coming between the first and third wonderful parts of the threefold work of grace which God does for us. We have seen the final thing, that is, when we are glorified at the coming of our Lord Jesus. We have seen the beginning of it in the passages just read—that is, when we were justified. We are *going* to be glorified, by God's grace. We *have been* justified, by God's grace; and we didn't have anything to do with accomplishing it. It was finished. We just believed God. He did it all. But what about the meantime, between the first and the last, between the beginning and the end? What is the justified

Christian going to do while he waits for his glorification? True, his glorification may be blessedly near. Praise God, the signs of the times look so! But we may have an hour yet to live before the Lord comes. And what about the hour? The Christian isn't left untempted. The Christian is the shining mark for Satan: and is there no hope, has grace no message for us in the meantime, right now, between the wonderful beginning and the wonderful ending? Is there no hope for us in the matter of present sin through the grace, the unaided work, of God?

Yes, thank God, there is! There is just as much hope for this middle time as for the ending and as for the beginning; and it is just as truly God's grace. In Romans 5:10 we read: "For if, when we were enemies"—we were enemies, too, dead in trespasses and sins—"we were reconciled to God by the death of his Son, much more, being reconciled"—having been justified—"we shall be saved by his life." Or as Bishop Moule has rendered that, "We shall be kept safe in His life." A moment-by-moment experience. We were saved by His death; now in the meantime, in this present time, if we but believe, we shall be kept safe (from the power of sin) in His life. And that means His resurrection life. That is the whole message of Romans 6, walking in newness of life, moment by moment, while we are waiting for our resurrection bodies, having the joy of the resurrection life. As Paul says in Romans 5:17, "For if by one man's offence death reigned by one; much more they which receive abundance of grace and of the gift of righteousness"—not the "work of righteousness" but the "gift of righteousness"; it's an outright gift—"shall reign in life" now and here "by one, Jesus Christ."

That is the middle part. Grace can keep us safe in His life. Grace puts us on the throne and keeps us reigning in victory over sin now and here. And then that wonderful verse in Romans 6:14! I don't know whether there is a more blessed verse anywhere! "Sin shall not have dominion over you: for ye are . . . under grace." You are not under law, which says, "Do," but you are under grace, which says, "Done"; for grace excludes works from having anything to do with this freedom from the dominion of sin.

Yes, praise God, there *is* a message for the "meantime." It has been a pretty mean time, a dark "meantime," in the lives of some of us Christians; but it can be a blessed and glorious meantime—a golden mean between the beginning and the end. It will be a glorious time between our justification and our glorification, if we will but take it on the same terms that we take the beginning and the end.

Grace! Simple faith! Colossians 2:6 (A.S.V.) tells the whole secret: "As therefore ye received Christ Jesus the Lord, so walk in him." That is very plain. While we are still in these bodies of corruption, while we are still assaulted by every fiery dart of the evil one—and he surely knows how to assult—we are to walk in Christ. But how? Just as we received Him. And how did we receive Christ? By setting our teeth and saying, "There, thank God, I am going to help Him get me born again"? No! We received Him by faith. We received Him as the gift of God. That's the way we are to walk. "As ye received Christ Jesus the Lord, so walk in him."

You didn't know I was going to give you theology, but I have been doing so. Justification at the beginning, glorification at the end, and in the meantime sanctification. Don't be afraid of the word sanctification! It's a Bible word. There are all sorts of perverted and unscriptural teachings about it, but, thank God, grace sanctifies us. Grace is going to glorify us. And grace, if we let it, sanctifies us experimentally, moment by moment, unaided by any efforts of ours. For grace is the exclusive work of God.

But let us forget all about theology—although theology has its real place—and rather let us "remember Jesus Christ." *He* is all the theology we need in this practical matter of the victorious life, of walking in the resurrection life. First Corinthians 1:30, 31 settles all that. "Of him," not of yourself, not of your works, but of Him; and this is preceded by the statement that no flesh should glory in His presence: "But of him are ye in Christ Jesus, who of God is made unto us wisdom, and righteousness, and sanctification, and redemption." Christ is your sanctification and your redemption. There is a glory that is coming—"That, according as it is written, He that glorieth, let him glory in the Lord." Glory in the Lord, in what He has done for you, and is doing for you, and will do for you; not in what you do for God.

As someone once said at the Keswick Convention, we Christians all know that we are justified by faith, but somehow we have gotten the idea that, for sanctification, we must paddle our own canoe. Praise God, we don't have to paddle our own canoe for anything that the grace of God offers. "Thanks be to God, who giveth us the victory through our Lord Jesus Christ." I believe that the word we most need to emphasize in 1 Corinthians 15:57 is the word *"giveth."* We talk about the grace of God, but forget that the victory is *given* to us. You don't have to work for a gift, neither do you have any share in buying a gift. The whole thing is given to you, exclusive of your efforts and work.

As I have already said, the first twenty-five years of my Christian life I lived in utter ignorance of this simple truth. I can never forget the 14th of August, 1910, when the scales dropped from my eyes, and I saw that Christ was my life. Christ was my victory. I wasn't bothering about the theological questions that have been discussed to the entanglement and defeating of so many Christians. I had never even heard of the question of "eradication," for example; I didn't know there was such a question. And I don't care about it today. I have gotten to the place where I have lost my interest in the question of *how* God *does* things. That is His business, not mine. But I do know *that* God *does* this thing; and I know it not because of any experiences of victory God has given me—blessed though some of them have been, and beyond anything I dreamed possible; but I know it *because* God *says* so. I don't know it by looking at my own victories, or at the victories of others. I don't know it because of any present experience or consciousness of Christ that I have. I know it because the Word of God says it. He says, "Sin shall not have dominion over you," and, if that is not true, God is a liar; and if that is not true, I have no hope of salvation, I have no hope of anything. But God is *not* a liar: He is the eternal truth; and because His Word is true, it means that God is responsible for my victory; and, until I doubt Him, I am going to have victory. The moment I begin to waver and doubt, down I go, into the sea of doubt, as Peter did when he got his eyes off Christ.

I shall never forget a fortnight that I had the privilege of spending in the Moody Bible Institute, several years ago. One day a student came to my room and said he was being defeated by sin. He told me what that sin was in his own life—a sin that gets into the lives of so many men.

"Of course you have surrendered everything to the Lord?" I asked.

"Oh yes," he answered, "I think so."

"Is there anything you wouldn't do for Him?"

"No," he replied, "nothing–except, I think, I never could do open air evangelistic work in a Roman Catholic community."

Well, I shouldn't have thought of suggesting that as a test question! He went on: "I was brought up in a Roman Catholic community, and it would be very difficult for me to do work among them."

"Suppose the Lord Jesus should come right into this room," I suggested, "and tell you that was just what He wanted you to do. Would you do it?"

Honest fellow that he was, he answered, "I don't know whether I would or not."

"Then let's settle that first, before we talk about victory," I urged, and we went to our knees together. And on his knees that man surrendered that one detail of his life plans that he had been keeping from Christ. He had come to the Moody Institute to study to be an evangelist; but he had been perhaps unconsciously saying of that one thing, "Lord, you won't ask me to do *that*." Of course he couldn't have victory. But now he turned over *all* his life plans to the Lord. He surrendered everything. And he got up from his knees victorious. We didn't have to spend any more time on the subject. His face was full of victory. He hadn't done anything except Romans 12:1. He had yielded his very being a living sacrifice to God. And if any of you dear people here are making life plans for yourselves, you must stop it—if you want victory. It isn't your job; God made your life plans before the foundation of the world. He just wants you to yield yourself to Him, and He'll take care of your life plans. Surrender completely and unconditionally, or you'll never have victory. That's the first point in victory.

For the second—well, I remember how, toward the close of the two weeks there, a young women student came to me with a distressed face and a heavy heart. "I have been listening," she said, "to what has been said about victory and peace and power, and all the rest of it, and I am longing for it, but I can't get it." Then she went on: "I am finishing my work here this summer; I am going out into the field of evangelism. But if I don't get what you are talking about, I shall feel that my entire course at Moody Institute will have been a failure, and I dare not go out into the work."

We talked together about the simple

matter of surrender and faith, first giving yourself wholly to God, and then just believing that God is doing His part. Said she, "I know it is just a question of faith, but I *haven't got that faith*. That's the thing that's keeping me out. I can't seem to get the faith for victory."

"Are you saved?" I asked her.

"Oh, yes," she said.

"What makes you think you are saved?"

"Why," she said, "I know I am; John 3:16 settles that. God has told us that anyone who believes on Jesus as Saviour is saved."

"You believe that, do you?" I asked.

"Why, certainly; I just take it on the Word of God."

"Well, then," I answered, "you have all the faith you need, and you are using it. For it's the faith that you are already using and have used for years for your salvation that is the only faith you need for victory."

"Do you mean that?" she exclaimed. "Is it just the same as salvation?"

"Exactly the same," I answered. And her burden dropped then and there; and in the days that followed she praised God that the faith she already had, and had had all the time, was the only faith she needed.

After all, it was just a simple recognition of God's *faithfulness*. So let us forget all about our faith, and think only of God's faithfulness to us through Christ Jesus. A year or so later I had a letter from that woman, and she told me what a wonderful year of service she had had. "Oh, Mr. Trumbull," she wrote, "as you have occasion to speak to people about the victorious life, won't you tell them that the faith they need for victory is the same faith that they have for salvation." Praise God, if you believe in Jesus as your Saviour, you've got all the faith you need, all the faith the Apostle Paul had! You don't need more faith. You need simply to use the faith you have. There was a rebuke our Lord once gave His disciples, when they asked Him to increase their faith. "Increase it!" He said, "Why, faith the size of a mustard seed will do."

If we have any faith at all—I mean, if we believe God is faithful — let us quietly cease from our works and stop trying to win the victory.

As someone has said, we are not fighting to win a victory; we are celebrating the victory that has been won.

Will you thank the Lord Jesus now for having won your Victory—and rest the whole case there, on His grace?

6

IS – THE SECRET OF VICTORY

A fact is often a more useful thing, for immediate needs, than a promise. That is why God has given us, in His Word, so many clear statements concerning facts that we need to know, along with His precious promises.

It is a very precious truth, on the one hand, that if we ask God, in the name of the Lord Jesus, to do certain things, He will do them. He has pledged His word to us for this, and He is the truth: He keeps His word. But there are certain circumstances in which it is even more valuable for us to know, not that He *will* do a certain thing if we ask Him, but that He *is* doing it anyway, and therefore we do not even need to ask Him. God's promise to do, upon our request, is one rich part of our Christian Life; but there is a sense in which certain facts that God declares are so, whether we ask or not, make an even richer part of our life.

At a series of meetings on the Victorious

Life, held in Toronto, the speaker told of the way of deliverance from certain temptations that come like a flash of lightning in their instantaneous unexpectedness, when there is not time to pray or ask the Lord for deliverance. At such times our safety lies, not in a prayer for deliverance, for there is not time for that, but rather in the *fact* that Christ *is* delivering us without our asking Him; and in such an instant, as always, we are to *thank* our Lord for deliverance, not ask Him for it. For the Lord does not say to us, "My grace will be sufficient for thee whenever thou askest for it." He says, "My grace *is* sufficient for thee." That wonderful word is not a promise: it is a statement of fact.

Some time after the meetings the speaker received a letter from a Christian worker in Toronto, who has for years known about the truth of victory by faith, yet who had been unsatisfied and hungry in his spiritual life. Now he wrote: "Your word of illustration about the fraction of a second being insufficient for the framing of a prayer touched the point of my difficulty. The great big IS goes with me as my guardian, and I am experiencing something new. You know my head troubles me so that I can go to but few meetings and do little evening work, and my nerves have been frazzled and jangling; but I know He can and will take care of the 'things that crop up suddenly.' " Yes, He will do this because He *is* doing this.

That little two-letter verb "IS" in our Lord's wonderful word to Paul and through him to every member of the body of Christ, "My grace is sufficient for thee," is a veritable rock of ages. The writer of this editorial, finding marvelous strength and safety and deliverance in it, was turning it over in his mind one day, and thinking of the sufficiency of Christ. He was clinging to, or rather resting on, that word "is"—and then he thought to himself: "But have I any right to make so prominent that meaningless little verb 'is,' and depend so much upon it, when it seems as though I ought to think rather of some more important word, like the name of Christ?"

Instantly there flashed into his mind what it seems must have been the reply of the Holy Spirit Himself: "But the verb 'is' is the same verb as that which God says is His own name, 'I AM.' And if that little word 'is' is part of the very name of God Himself, you need not fear to think a great deal of it and rest confidently and wholly upon it."

Praise God for His wonderful name! Praise God that He *is!* The man of victorious faith simply believes that God is, and that all that God says is so, *is* so. To believe this pleases God; for "without faith it is impossible to be well-pleasing unto him; for he that cometh to God must believe that he is, and that he is a rewarder of them that seek after him" (Heb. 11:6, A.S.V.).

Think, for a moment, of the meaning of the name "LORD," or Jehovah. When Moses asked God what name he should use for Him to the Children of Israel, God replied: I AM THAT I AM: and he said, Thus shalt thou say unto the children of Israel, I AM hath sent me unto you" (Exod. 3:14). The word Lord, or Jehovah, means literally, "He that is who He is, therefore the eternal I AM." Other elements entering into the name Jehovah give us, as its meaning, "The self-existent One who reveals Himself." And this name Lord or Jehovah is preeminently God's redemption name. It is used in Bible passages which specially refer to the redeeming and saving work that God does for fallen, sinful man.

It is no accident, surely, that a central, vital word in that marvelous statement of fact, "My grace is sufficient for thee," is the little verb "is" which is a part of the very name and being and redemptive love of God. Jehovah God, our Redeemer God in His marvelous covenant relations with us, is the eternal Christ, slain from the foundation of the world, whose outpoured life is the grace of God working omnipotently in our behalf, without our asking, without our seeking, without any conditions. God *is,* whether we believe this or not. Christ's grace *is* sufficient for us, whether we believe it or not. But His grace cannot become experimentally effective in our lives so long as we make God a liar and say that what He declares to be a fact is not a fact. The moment we *believe* in this God-declared fact, there is a sufficiency of omnipotence successfully at work in our lives that makes us more than conquerors and leads us in triumph.

All of God's omnipotent sufficiency in His saving and delivering and keeping power for men is in Christ. Christ is more than a promise: He is a fact, the eternal Rock of Ages upon whom we may rest everything. God's grace is Christ; and the grace of God in Jesus Christ is *sufficient.* Are we thanking and praising Him for this?

The Toronto friend who is "experiencing something new" because he is resting on the fact of Christ's sufficiency, resting in Christ Himself the eternal "Is," has drawn a Bible bookmark showing that brief but all-sufficient text of 2 Corinthians 12:9. In its design the relative importance of that wonderful verb is plainly to be seen. Moreover, it is to be noted that the pronoun "My," referring to our Lord Jesus Christ, is much larger than the pronoun "thee." Even though your needs are terribly great, so great as to leave you hopeless, Christ and His grace are infinitely greater. "Where sin abounded, grace did much more abound" (Rom. 5:20). There is a blessing in the way the text is presented in this Bible bookmark, especially as printed in two colors, with that central verb "IS" in bright red, the color of the precious redeeming blood of our Lord Jesus.

It is worth while to repeat the familiar story, here, of the circumstances that revolutionized the life of one of the best known Christian ministers of Great Britain, whom God has made a tower of strength for the past forty-five years in giving the message of victory at the great Keswick Convention.

It was back in 1874 that a young Church of England vicar, the Rev. J. W. Webb-Peploe, with his wife, went to a seashore place with their youngest child, then a year old. At this place Mr. Webb-Peploe met Sir Arthur Blackwood, and when the older man learned the calling of the younger, he held his hand tightly as he asked, "Have you got 'rest'?"

"Yes, I hope so," replied the young minister.

"What do you mean by that?" came the further question.

"That my sins are all forgiven through the blood of Jesus Christ, and that He will take me Home to Heaven when I die."

"Yes, but what about the time between? Have you rest in all your work as a clergyman, and in your parish troubles?"

"No, I wish I had," said the young minister honestly.

"I want the same," said Sir Arthur; "and today the great Oxford Convention begins. [The Oxford Convention was the forerunner of the Keswick Convention.] Mrs. Trotter is going to write to me every day an account of the meetings; you and I can meet and pray that God will give us the blessing of *the rest of faith* which they are going to speak of there. God is not confined to Oxford."

For three days the two men met together, and then Mr. Webb-Peploe's little child was suddenly taken away by the

Heavenly Father. The young earthly father took the little body home, and reached there much wounded in feeling through contact with people who did not understand his circumstances. After the funeral, he began to prepare a sermon to preach to his people. He took for his text the passage found in the lesson for the day, 2 Corinthians 12:9—"My grace is sufficient for thee." He spent some two hours in working on the sermon, and then he said to himself: "It is not true; I do not find it sufficient under this heavy trouble that has befallen me." And his heart cried out to God to *make* His grace sufficient for his hour of sore need and crushing sorrow.

As he wiped the tears away from his eyes he glanced up and saw over his study table an illuminated text-card that his mother had given him. The words read, "My grace is sufficient for thee," the word "is" being in bold type and in a different color from all the other words in the text. And Prebendary Webb-Peploe said forty years later, as he told the incident, that he seemed to hear a voice saying to him: "You fool, how dare you ask God to *make* what *is?* Believe His word. Get up and trust Him, and you will find it true at every point." He took God at His word, he

believed the *fact*, and his life was revolutionized. He entered into such an experience
of rest and peace, such trust in a sufficient
Saviour, as he never before had dreamed
could be possible. Within a month the
governess in the family said to Mrs. Webb-
Peploe, "The farmers are remarking how
much changed the vicar is: he does not seem
fretful any more, but seems to be quiet and
gentle about everything." And from that day
to this, now forty-five years later, many
another has praised God that the life of this
minister of the Gospel is a testimony to the
sufficiency of the grace which God declares
is a fact.

The secret of victory is not praying, but
praising: not asking, but thanking. All eternity will not be long enough to finish
praising and thanking our Lord Jesus Christ
for the simple, glorious fact that His grace IS
sufficient for us.

"CHRIST WHO IS OUR LIFE"

"I **AM**." *Who* art Thou, Lord?
 I Am—all things to thee;
Sufficient to thine every need;
 Thou art complete in Me.

I Am –thy Peace, thy Joy,
  Thy Righteousness, thy Might;
I Am –thy Victory o'er sin,
  Thy Keeper day and night.

I Am–thy Way, thy Life;
  I Am–the Word of Truth;
Whate'er thy lack, I Am–to thee
  El Shaddai, Enough.

I Am–thy Life within.
  Thine Everlasting Bread;
Eat of my Flesh, drink of my Blood,
  I Am–What dost thou need?

—Adah Richmond

7

PERILS OF THE VICTORIOUS LIFE

In the truly Victorious Life the Christian believer, having put on the whole armor of God (Eph. 6:11), moves forward under the protection of the shield of faith, wherewith he is able to quench *all* the fiery darts of the Evil One (v. 16). God's Word is absolute on the completeness of the victory that is the experience of every child of God who trusts that victory wholly to Christ. It is not a once-for-all victory; it is a moment-by-moment victory, had each moment only in the present, but had completely in that present as the believer "looks away" from all else "unto Jesus," the author and perfecter of our faith (Heb. 12:2).

But what a perilous life it is! Satan hates it; for it is an incarnate advertisement of the sufficiency of his Conqueror, Jesus Christ. Therefore to trust Christ for complete victory is to be moved up into the front line trench of the Christian warfare; and front line trenches are perilous places when the attack is on. There is no life in the world so perilous as the Victorious Life. And there is no life so safe. Where the onslaughts of the Adversary are the most terrific, the grace of the Captain of our salvation is the most effectively demonstrated.

Some of the perils are so subtle, so unexpected, that they may not be recognized unless we frankly face them in advance as terribly real possibilities—nay, not possibilities, but certainties. We need a supernaturally sensitized consciousness of these perils if we would be safeguarded.

For, as has been iterated and reiterated by all who know anything of real victory in Christ, the Victorious Life is not the untempted life, but it is the most tempted life that anyone can live. Our Lord was tempted, and the "servant is not greater than his Lord" (John 13:16). Indeed, it may fairly be said that one never knows the full meaning of temptation until he has dared to trust Christ for full victory. Then come the temptations as never before: desperate, diabolical, hellish, subtle, refined, gross, spiritual, fleshly—the whole gamut of all the deception and the downpull that the world, the flesh, and the Devil can bring to the soul of a child of God. But Christ sees them all, and He is standing on sentry-guard in our lives against them; the Word of God has disclosed them all to us, and this "sword of the Spirit" (Eph. 6:17) is our sure weapon today as it was our Lord's in those victorious words, thrice repeated, "It is written" (Matt. 4:4, 7, 10).

The secret of complete victory is faith: simply believing that *Jesus has done and is doing it all.* Victory is entered upon by a single act of faith, as is salvation. Victory is maintained by the attitude of faith. But suppose the believer, having experienced the miracle of victory over sin through trusting his Lord's sufficiency, comes, somehow, to doubt that sufficiency? At once his victory is broken, and he fails. This is possible at any moment. And at once, if there should be failure through unbelief, comes a real peril. The lie of Satan is whispered in the ear, "You have sinned; and that proves that you never had the blessing you thought you had: you never had the Victorious Life." This is a lie, of course, as are most of Satan's attacks. They say at Keswick, "If you *should* fail, shout Victory!" Not with any idea of denying the reality of the failure, but in recognition of the fact that *Jesus* has not failed, and that there may be instantaneous and complete restoration through faith in His unimpaired sufficiency.

The peril just here is, either that we shall think we never had the blessing we thought we had; or that we shall imagine it will now take us some time to get back into the blessing. Satan may tell us that we cannot have complete victory again until we have gone apart alone with the Lord for a day, or an hour, or five minutes. But our Lord wants us to believe Him for instaneous cleansing and restoration. The way back is as "it is written": "If we confess our sins, he is faithful and righteous to forgive us our sins, and to cleanse us from all unrighteousness" (1 John 1:9). The confession can be unspoken, in the instant turning of the heart to God and claiming of cleansing. Every moment of delay in believing Him for this is further sin, grieving and wounding His loving heart.

Another peril is twofold: our supposing, on the one hand, that the longer we continue in victory the safer we are; and, on the other hand, that if by sin we have broken our victory we are thereby weaker, and less certain of continued victory. Both ideas are perilous and fallacious.

This is quickly seen when we recognize

that Christ, and Christ alone, is our Victory.
Suppose we should live for ten years in
unbroken victory; that ten years' record of
unbroken victory does not add a particle to
the strength of our Lord Jesus Christ; it does
not increase the sufficiency of His grace, for
that sufficiency is infinite. The assurance of
our continuance in victory is not our good
record in victory, but the grace of our Lord.
Our Lord and His grace are the same
yesterday, and today, and forever (Heb.
13:8). We have *all* His infinite grace at work
for us and in us any moment and every
moment. Therefore our continued record in
victory adds nothing to our assurance of
victory, for it adds nothing to Christ, and He
alone is our assurance of victory. Of ourselves we are just as weak and helpless, just
as sinful, just as impotent for victory after
ten years' unbroken victory as we were the
first moment after being born again into the
family of God. Even the veteran warrior in
the Victorious Life is always capable of
unbelief and of disastrous defeat in sin. He
needs the moment-by-moment looking away
unto Jesus as His only Saviour just as much
as the young Christian who has just entered
upon that life.

And so of failure: my unbelief and

resulting sin do not weaken my Lord at all. Having confessed that sin and having been cleansed and restored by Him, He is just as strong, just as omnipotent, as though I had never failed. And my victory now, after failure, depends wholly upon His sufficient and omnipotent grace, which is the same yesterday, today, and forever.

We shall be safeguarded from these two perils, of overconfidence through continued victory, and of weakening fear through failure, if we remember God's Word concerning the absoluteness of the victory that is ours in Christ. That victory is not a relative thing, not a comparative thing, not a matter of degree at all: it is the freedom with which the Son sets men free (John 8:36). Not that we are given "sinless perfection." We always have our sinful nature, which can sin and will sin any moment that we fail to trust Christ for His victory in us. But as we trust Him, His victory in us is absolute.

The very joy of the yielded life, when God's will is wholly accepted, brings with it another peril. It has been said that when Satan finds he cannot prevent one from doing the whole will of God, he then tries to drive that one beyond the will of God. And it is a perilous thing to go beyond the will of

God, even in matters that of themselves are right.

It often happens, for example, that the Victorious Life Christian is driven beyond the will of God into imaginary duties. Satan comes as an angel of light (2 Cor. 11:14), suggesting that the believer do this or that thing, good in itself but not the will of God for that one. The believer has found great blessing in listening to the voice of the Holy Spirit, and in instant obedience to His leadings; and when Satan speaks, giving leadings in directions that of themselves are entirely right, the unsuspecting believer follows those leadings, no blessing results, and then follow anxiety, confusion, perhaps doubt and fog.

God prompts us, for example, to speak to this or that one about Jesus as Saviour. We do so, and we have the joy of leading a soul into salvation.

Now comes Satan with the insistent suggestion that we speak to one and another, under all sorts of circumstances and at all times, about salvation or victory. We follow the impulse, which is not of God, and no blessing follows. A soul-winning Christian had a "leading" to go to a certain street and number in the city where he lived and to talk

with the persons there about Christ as their
Saviour. The house was one of which he
knew nothing, but he went. He rang the bell,
and after some time of waiting he found that
it was an unoccupied house. That leading
was evidently not from God. The resulting
confusion and doubt in that young man's
mind are easy to see.

It is possible to fall into confusion again,
as to confession of sin. Perhaps we have
confessed to a fellow Christian some personal sin or failure of our own, and real
blessing has resulted, both to that one and to
ourselves. Then the suggestion comes to us
that, inasmuch as that confession was so
blessed, we must now confess to some fellow
Christian every sin that we recognize, perhaps some sins that were long ago put away,
forgiven, and cleansed by our Lord, or every
present failure or mistake of any sort. And
the obsession of confession takes hold of us,
and into the fog we go. God does not want
this. God will guide us as to when He may
wish a confession made to another; and He
will guide us as to when to let it be a matter
wholly between Himself and ourselves. One
general principle here is that it is to be kept
to God and ourselves unless someone else
will be injured by our withholding confes-

sion. If a confession to another or to others will accomplish nothing except giving them a knowledge of our sin, it is to be questioned whether God would have such confession made.

Or again, having surrendered the whole life to the mastery of the Lord, having given up the pride of the flesh, all luxuries and self-gratification, there is the peril of asceticism. Perhaps fine clothes, or jewelry, or overindulgence in food were among the things that had to go when we surrendered wholly to the Lord. As we find our new joy in Him, not in these things, we may be driven beyond the will of God into an asceticism that dishonors Him. More than one wholly surrendered Christian has mistakenly become indifferent and careless about personal attire or appearance, and has actually become repellent to others because of this mistake. Or, having been delivered from the sin of luxury in jewelry, we may be driven beyond the will of God into supposing that every bit of gold or silver we have should now be given away or sold and the proceeds given directly to the Lord's service. Christian women have actually sold their wedding rings under this form of sadly mistaken asceticism. The spirit is commendable, but neither the guidance nor the results are necessarily of God.

We are to maintain a golden mean between the extremes of asceticism and luxury. We are to take care of our personal appearance, our cleanliness, our clothing, so as to be attractive to our fellow men; it is a positive duty to be attractive Christians, both in dress and in appearance, that others may be won to us in order that we may win them to our Lord. We are to do all things to the glory of God (1 Cor. 10:31).

This includes our pleasures as well as all else. We are not to believe the lie of Satan that everything that is pleasurable or attractive is sinful. We are to enjoy our meals, for example, not reduce them to the minimum of mere physical sustenance. And so of other temporal details of our life.

We may get the mistaken idea that when we have a choice between something that is hard and something that is easy, the hard thing is always God's will. His will may be just the opposite. There is not necessarily any virtue in difficulty, and there is not necessarily any sin in ease. The only question is, What is God's will for us in each matter that comes before us?

"Beloved, believe not every spirit, but

prove the spirits, whether they are of God"
(1 John 4:1). And we are never to abandon
our God-given common sense in the Victorious Life.

Here is one way of distinguishing
between God's leadings and Satan's "angel of
light" leadings. To the really surrendered
Christian, who is trusting Christ for victory,
God's leadings and promptings never nag, or
worry, or harass. Satan's do just this. If one
has a seeming "leading" to do something
that in itself is good, yet with the impulse
there is a sense of nagging disquiet, almost as
though a mosquito or a gnat were buzzing
about to try to drive us in a certain
direction, that is Satan's earmark, his calling
card; and his false "leading" is to be instantly recognized and rejected. The Holy
Spirit's leadings to the surrendered and
trusting Christian come with a sense of peace
and quiet, even if they point in a really
difficult direction which only the grace of
God can enable one to follow.

DO NOT DEPEND ON EXPERIENCES

The Victorious Life is a supernatural life:
it is a living miracle, a thrilling adventure, for
it is God's work and God's working. Our

early experiences in the life of victory are likely to be so different from anything we have known before, so out of the ordinary in supernatural demonstration of God's grace and power,that at once we are plunged into a peril.

That peril is that we mistakenly suppose we must continually be having thrilling, unexpected, supernatural evidences of God's power. And if these supernatural phenomena do not occur, we are tempted to think that something is wrong.

Now God wants us to trust, not in supernatural experiences, but in Himself. It is for *Him* to decide when the unusual shall come into our life, and when our life shall be commonplace and humdrum so far as things of sight and sense are concerned. It would seem to be a safe statement that it is God's purpose that the "supernatural," so far as circumstances and experiences are concerned, should be the unusual rather than the usual in the life of His wholly trusting children. (Of course we remember that victory over sin is itself supernatural, and that God expects us to live in continual victory over sin, which means that our life in that respect is to be continually supernatural, always the "life that is Christ." This is apart

from the question of the supernatural experiences or phenomena that are often granted
to us in our ministry in His name.) And so
He would deliver us from the peril of testing
Him, or testing our victory, by circumstances
or manifestations, and rather He asks us to
trust "just Himself."

It has been well said that everyone needs
two conversions: first, from the natural to
the supernatural; and second, from the
supernatural to the natural.

Let us be delivered, also, from the peril
of unconsciously assuming an infallible
knowledge of God's will. God's leadings may
be so blessed and so unmistakable that, as we
testify to others about them, we speak of
how "God said this to me," or "God led me
to do that." And then, if we are not on our
guard, we thoughtlessly slip into habitual
expressions about God's leading us. Some
true and yielded Christians almost never
speak of any action or decision of theirs
without prefacing it with the words that God
told them to do this or that. And quite often
in the experience of such a one later circumstances show plainly that God did not tell
them to do this or that, but that they had
misunderstood His leading, as is possible at
any time for any believer, even while wholly
yielded.

There is an unconscious assumption of infallibility in that expression which can become really unconscious cant. Is it not better, instead of saying, "God told me to do this," to say, "I believe God would have me do this"? Let us recognize that we *may* be mistaken. Even if we are quite certain in our own hearts and minds of what God's leading is, it is not well to claim infallible knowledge, without qualification, in our conversation with others.

The blessings that Christ gives us in the Victorious Life—in the ninefold "fruit of the Spirit" (Gal. 5:22, 23), for example—are so wonderful that we are in danger of thinking more about the blessings than of the Blesser. Joy becomes such a wonderful experience— the supernatural joy which nothing can defeat, which is independent of all circumstances and environment—that we may, without realizing it, come to think more of this "joy of our Lord" than we do of our Lord Himself. He wants us to worship, not the fruit of the Spirit, but the Spirit. There is a needed reminder in the saying that is attributed to Spurgeon: "I looked at Jesus, and the dove of peace flew into my heart. I looked at the dove of peace, and she flew away."

The Christian who is wholly trusting the
Lord for victory soon realizes that many
Christians about him have not seen the truth
of victory, and are not thus trusting Christ.
He may be in close contact with Christians
who are older, much farther along in many
ways, yet not living in the victory-secret that
is so precious to him. And then comes the
peril of pride. Almost without realizing it the
Christian who knows Christ as victory can let
slip some word criticizing a fellow Christian
who is not in on the secret, or a condescend-
ing comment on such a one's mistake or
failure. "Holier than thou" is one of the
perils of the Victorious Life. Of course the
instant one speaks thus of another, or thinks
in his inmost heart thus of another, his
victory is gone; he has sinned. And we must
recognize this peril if we would be kept from
it. The Christian who is living in victory is *in
himself* no whit better than the carnal
Christian who is plainly sinning. The self-
nature of the two is identical: hopelessly
sinful. The only good thing about the victorious Christian is Christ; and we deserve no
credit for Christ: the glory and honor and
victory are all His. True victory, therefore,
must keep us humble: and it will.

Yet it is a sad fact that more than one

young person, or older person, has gone away from a Victorious Life conference where the Lord was received in His fullness and victory was entered into, and has returned to the home church to speak disparagingly or critically of other Christians, even perhaps of the minister himself, who may not have seen and accepted the truth of victory by faith in Christ. This has brought the very preciousness of the message of victory into disrepute, has wounded the Lord in the house of His friends, and of course has made it well-nigh impossible to pass on the truth of victory to those who have not known it. The truly victorious Christian speaks of others always in humility, in keen consciousness of his own natural sinfulness and helplessness, and in that perfect love that is kind, vaunteth not itself, is not puffed up, doth not behave itself unseemly, taketh not account of evil, never faileth (1 Cor. 13:4-8).

Then there is the peril of being unteachable.

Here is one who has entered into victory through faith in Christ. At once there comes from the Holy Spirit a new illumination on God's Word, a new knowledge of things never before known, a new wisdom, unmistakable and directly from God. There is a flood of light on duties that were heretofore confused. He is able to counsel others as never before. All this is not imaginary; it is genuine and vital. And he praises God with gratitude unspeakable.

Then perhaps a fellow Christian criticizes him for something he has done or said, and says that it was not as it ought to be. This fellow Christian may not know Christ as victory at all, and the one who is criticized is keenly conscious of the fact that his critic has not the illumination and the victory that are his own. Now comes the peril: that this victorious Christian will say to himself about the other: "He cannot tell me anything about this. He does not know the secret of victory. The Bible has not been opened to him by the Holy Spirit as it has to me. He has not the light that I have." And so the heart is closed to the criticism, and the man has fallen into the peril of being unteachable. And all the time the criticism that has come to him from perhaps an unenlightened Christian is sound and true, and God sent it to him for his own guidance and blessing.

May God deliver us, in victory, from this subtle danger of unwillingness to learn from those who may indeed not be as far along in the Christian life as we are. Why, a completely victorious Christian can learn from the criticisms of unsaved, unregenerate people! And often he ought to. The Victorious Life is no guarantee of omniscience, of infallibility in knowledge. Humility of mind, eagerness to know any and every criticism that anyone may have concerning us, and then grateful acceptance of whatever truth there may be in that criticism (and there is pretty sure to be some truth in it), is our safeguarding against this peril of unconscious unwillingness to learn.

BEWARE OF PRESUMPTION AND COMPLACENCY

After one has recognized the peril of being driven beyond God's will, there comes the peril of sagging below God's will.

We see that victory is all of grace; that no works of our own are needed to accomplish it nor can possibly accomplish it. We rejoice that we have learned that we may "let God do it all," and He abundantly vindicates His pledge that He will as we trust Him.

And now comes the peril of presuming on God's grace: substituting presumption for faith, license for liberty.

We used to think that the more we studied the Bible the more victorious we should be. We used to think that the more time we spent in prayer the more victory we could have. We see now that even these good works cannot accomplish our victory, but that simple faith in the sufficiency of God's grace is the secret.

Very well, then, we are tempted to think, we need not be so careful now to take the same amount of time for our Bible study, or for our prayer life, because "Christ is doing it all." And down into defeat we go the moment we have been deceived by that lie of Satan. True, victory is by faith; but faith must be fed; and faith cannot be fed apart from daily nourishment from the Word of God, and daily time alone with God in prayer. The new experience of freedom from the power of sin through the sufficiency of Christ should result in *more* time with His Word, *more* time with Him in prayer, not less. We cannot know continuance in victory if we presume on God's grace and neglect our opportunities of fellowship with Him.

Never, *never,* NEVER during this life dare any Christian neglect the written Word of God. A young Christian who had seen Christ as Victory and was rejoicing in the new blessings of freedom and power was talking with a veteran Christian minister about it all. And this was the sound word the older man spoke: "Now keep close to the Word of God." And he went on to tell the younger man how, time after time in the history of the so-called "higher life" experience among Christians through the Christian centuries, one after another either of individuals or of groups of Christians had gone onto the rocks and down into wreck through supposing that they had, by Christ and the Holy Spirit within them, all that they needed, and could therefore safely pay little attention to the Bible.

We must not sag below God's will, moreover, in the ordinary duties of life in our relationships with our fellows. Those who have found the joy and blessing of the deep things of God are often careless in keeping appointments with their fellow men, careless about answering letters, careless about money matters—not involving honesty, but just exactness and thoughtfulness. The Christian who is trusting Christ for full victory dishonors Christ if he does not establish and maintain a reputation for being *utterly dependable,* in his contact with other human beings, *in every relationship.* Failure to keep an appointment on the minute, to be scrupulously exact in the fulfillment of every small as well as large obligation, cannot be excused on the ground that God's larger interests overrule the lesser matters. There are no "lesser matters" with God. The Holy Spirit is a Person of orderliness, and punctuality, and efficiency; if our lives are not conspicuous for this it is because He is not really allowed to control. God keeps sun and moon, earth and stars, moving in dependable and orderly ways; should we not let Him do as much for us who are members of the Body of Christ?

In every blessing there is a corresponding peril. In our knowledge of the marvelous blessing, for example, that our Lord will instantly forgive our sins and cleanse and restore us upon confession to Him and faith in Him, there is the peril that we may take sin too lightly: tolerate a break in our victory as though it were rather unimportant after all. Complacency in defeat is a peril of the Victorious Life. We would not say, doubtless, that we are willing to "sin that grace may abound" (Rom. 6:1); nevertheless we may unconsciously fall into that perilous attitude. More than one Christian who has known Christ as complete Victory will testify that, learning by experience the possibility of instant and complete restoration after failure, he began to tolerate breaks and failures in his life until they became the expected rather than the unexpected, the usual instead of the unusual; yes, even the habitual. Oh, there is tragedy then, indeed! And God may have to go deep with one who has thus played with God's grace before He can bring that one back again into habitual victory. Spiritual surgery may be necessary, of a kind that will cause an agony of suffering, before the cancer of "sinning that grace may abound" has been cut out. But, praise God, the Master Physician is ready and able for this, and after it has been done we shall praise Him that it was done, even though we may have thought He had cast us off while the operating and the hospital treatment were in progress. But why should we make it necessary for Him to do this? We need never lose our horror of sin, if in Christ we will see sin as He sees it, and hate it as the loathsome, hellish thing that it is.

While there will come to the victorious Christian temptations to subtle sin, refined sin, sin on a seemingly very high plane, the mystery of our sinful nature and of the wiles of the Adversary is such that even gross sin is

one of the perils of the Victorious Life. We
need not try to explain this; but history,
both in New Testament times and ever since,
abundantly declares it. There is something
about the life of spiritual power and victory
that, when broken into in the slightest way
by unbelief, seems to expose one most
terribly to sins of gross immorality and
degradation. Those who have gone highest
with the Lord can go lowest. Let us recognize this peril; let us confess this possibility
of our utterly sinful nature; and then let us
yield ourselves afresh to the mastery of our
holy Lord, and trust Him afresh for His
sufficiency to safeguard us from this awful
denial of His name and betrayal of our
stewardship.

The lesson from this particular peril is
that, after we have known the best Christ
offers us, to accept anything less than that
best for a single instant of time is to be in
deadly peril. If we *should* slip in any slightest
way, if we should find that sin has entered
through unbelief in our Lord's sufficiency,
let us instantly stop anything we are doing
and take the time necessary to confess to
Him, claim His forgiveness and entire cleansing, and trust Him at once for His complete
restoration and victory. Satan would like us

to think that because of what we may be doing just then for the Lord we must leave until later the matter of getting wholly back. If a failure has come toward the close of the day, perhaps after a hard day's work, when we are about ready to retire, the temptation will come that we are physically or mentally too weary now to think or pray this thing through, and we will get a good night's sleep and then let the Lord clear it all up in the morning. Deadly perilous is that. May God keep us from ever daring to go to sleep with unconfessed sin in our hearts, and in conscious loss of the victory that is ours in Christ. More than one Christian who has thus presumed on the grace of God has failed to let the Lord clear up everything in the morning, and has gone on into another day of defeat. *"Now* is the acceptable time" (2 Cor. 6:2), not only for salvation from the penalty of sin, but for salvation from its power, and restoration into that salvation if we have faithlessly denied our Lord. "Make me to walk on mine high places" (Hab. 3:19) is the only safe prayer and plane for the Christian who has ever known victory.

SOME FINAL PERILS
OF THE VICTORIOUS LIFE

It is perilous to look back at our best blessings of victory in Christ as though those best blessings were necessarily in the past. This is an almost inevitable temptation, because the new blessings of victory when one first trusts Christ for it are so new, so unexpected, so overwhelming and more than satisfying. And we may look longingly back at those first hours or days or months, and unconsciously suppose that we can never again have just the rich blessing we had then. This is to deny the sufficiency of God's grace, it is to deny that our Lord *is* "the same yesterday, and today, and forever."

And it is equally perilous to look to the future as the time when God's best blessings of victory for us are to be realized. God wants us to have His best *now*. To put that best either into the past or into the future is a peril that Satan will do his best to bring us into and keep us in. But the sufficiency of our Lord's grace, while it was true in the past and will be true in the future, is described by the Holy Spirit in the infallible Word of God as being in the present. "My grace *is* sufficient for thee," is His word (2 Cor. 12:9).

And the very name of our Jehovah-Jesus is "I *am*."

May just a word be spoken here as to another peril, that we may have a sensible recognition of this and be safeguarded accordingly? It is as to the relationship of men and women in the spiritual life. In general, it is evident from the Word of God as to the marriage relation, and from experience and observation and common sense, that the deeper spiritual relationships between fellow Christians should observe the same lines that the ordinary conventionalities of life insist upon: that is, that the deeper spiritual relationships should be between men and men, and between women and women, rather than between two persons of opposite sex—unless indeed God is bringing together two such persons that their lives may be united in marriage.

Not that there should be any unnaturalness in this, or any unhealthy self-consciousness when men and women, older or younger, properly talk together or pray together about their Lord and their possessions in their Lord. But Satan as an angel of light may lead on through their spiritual fellowship two such persons into a spiritual intimacy and a spiritual dependence upon each other which is not of God, and which can lead to unhappiness in more than one life, or real disaster.

Finally, let us recognize the peril of being unhuman—not inhuman, but un-human—because of the depth and intensity of our spiritual life. Not to be "human" is not of the Lord. We are living not only a spiritual life, but a bodily life as well; and we are living among those who also are in human bodies, in a world of rightful temporal interests as well as eternal interests. Let us not make the mistake of so living that persons shall say of us, as they have some, that we have a deep interest in others' souls, but none at all in their bodies. Let us be human. Let us be kind. Let us deliberately make it our business to cultivate certain secular, human interests, that we may have points of contact with the many round about us who know nothing of the spiritual interests that are so precious to us.

Some of the greatest spiritual leaders, some of the most blessedly used ambassadors of Christ, have had hobbies, such as nature-study, music, or something else of that sort, which God has blessed to them and to others. Such a hobby keeps one in touch with the present-day wonderful world which

God made. It gives one "bait" which he can use to catch the interest of another, and through that "bait" bring that other to Christ and to victory.

We are not to be afraid of healthy amusements of the right sort. If we go with a friend to see or play a tennis match or a baseball game, if we are watching or playing a game of checkers, let us not take it in such a way that everyone shall see that it has no real interest to us, and we are just making a concession to the earthly interests of our unenlightened friends, and patiently waiting until we can give our time to the really worthwhile things. This is not victory. It may sound harsh to call it asceticism and even priggishness; but that is the way it will seem to others, perhaps rightly so.

God wants to deliver us all the time from the peril of narrowness in the Victorious Life. If we have any musical ability, let us praise God for it and let us ask Him prayerfully to enable us to cultivate that ability that He may use our music to His glory. And this does not mean that we shall play or sing only hymns, either. There is plenty of other music that is not of the Devil, and that God would use to keep us close to our fellows in a joyous, healthy way.

Let us be very careful, too, about social courtesies. Christian people whose life-interests are wrapped up in the deeply spiritual are often criticized for carelessness about the little courtesies and attentions of their social relationships with others. This must not be; it dishonors our Lord. The Christian who is trusting Christ for victory should not be one whit less careful than is the man of the world or the society woman about those little niceties of life that betoken good breeding, good manners, true gentleness, and unselfish thoughtfulness for others. "The King's business" never requires discourtesy or lack of proper attentiveness to our fellows.

Moreover, let us not be deceived by letting the great needs of the outside world or of the church of Christ make such demands upon our time and energies that we are taken too much away from the loved ones in the home circle whom God has entrusted to us as our own supremely precious stewardship. Husbands and wives who have found Christ as their victory are often so eager to share this blessing with the greatest possible number that they unconsciously neglect the home—the children or the married partner—upon whom God would have them lavish their love and testimony and care beyond all others. Christians rejoicing in Christ as Victory sometimes need to "learn first to show piety towards their own family," remembering that "if any provideth not for his own, and specially his own household, he hath denied the faith, and is worse than an unbeliever" (1 Tim. 5:4, 8).

The Victorious Life is the only all-around life on earth. It is lived by body, mind, and spirit: in all three victoriously; and it touches our fellow beings at proper points of contact with their bodies, minds, and spirits.

We shall need to be ever and always on our guard, sensitively awake to the approach of the enemy in all the thousand-and-one ways by which he will seek to find a cleft in our armor. But—and here is another peril to be avoided—we are not to think more of Satan than of Christ. We are to recognize the terrible reality of Satan; we are to study the Word of God about our Adversary, that we may know all that God wants us to know about him; and then we are to look away from Satan unto Jesus; for "amid all these things we are more than conquerors through him who has loved us," and "to God be the

thanks who in Christ ever heads our tri-
umphal procession, and by our hands waves
in every place that sweet incense, the knowledge of him" (Weymouth, Rom. 8:37; 2 Cor.
2:14).